LOVE OF LIFE

Also by Donald W. Grant

Poetry

Shades of Life
Echoes of Life
Silence of Life
Reflections of Life
Trials of Life
Ecstasy of Life
Realities of Life

Essays

M.A.G.A.: Making America Go Awry

LOVE OF LIFE
A COLLECTION OF POEMS

DONALD W. GRANT

D/C
Perspectives

ISBN: 978-1-943142-68-2

Contents

— LOVE OF LIFE

A SOLUTION

Haters seem to always hate
    we seem unable to agree to disagree

does this have to be our fate?
    does this make you better than me?

we are divided, red state, blue state
    we don't see eye to eye debating, endlessly

does this have to be our fate?
    does this make you better than me?

there is a solution, somewhat out of date
    to love one another, yes, that old cliché

love can change our fate
    love can be the new reality.

A SIMPLE PLEDGE

I
meaning myself as an individual in a society

Pledge
as in making a solemn promise willingly

Allegiance
giving to the larger group my loyalty

To the flag
knowing this is a symbol of this country

of the United States of America
not divided, not choosing sides, not one party

and to the Republic
a represented government, not simply a democracy

. . .

for which it stands
> reminding us it is a symbol to be taken seriously

one Nation
> so many parts like a puzzle together in harmony

under God
> which I accept if not taken too seriously

with liberty
> a state of being free from restrictions placed on me

and justice
> that which is right or fair morally

for all
> the key to making all of the above a reality

AN EXPERT

Having or involving authoritative knowledge.

Who would have thought I would be an expert
    on getting a shot.

Typhoid, tetanus, malaria,
    yellow fever, smallpox, diphtheria-
    fourteen at the age of nine.

pick an arm, either one is fine

Polio fortunately came in sugar cubes,
    the rest, needles or should I say tubes.
    Shots back in the day hurt going in,
    arms sore for days, mine too thin.

Thank God for modern science
    needles so thin, not even a wince.

. . .

Especially with Covid-19
    two doses to complete the vaccine.

Lifesaving, and I didn't feel a thing,
    now just an expert on simply living.

BLACK

I t is as black
    as the most evil heart
    a heart filled with deceit,
lies, and pure ice.

it is as black
    as a night without
    a moon or stars, or
    the glow of city lights.

it is as black
    as the ink secreted
    by the squid, an ink
    without blends of cyan,
    magenta, or yellow.

it is as black
    as the deepest cave
    where only bats can see
    or the deepest ocean
    where light does not exist

. . .

it is as black
    as the center of a black hole
    spiraling thru space feeding
    on anything nearby

so, one might ask, why then
    do I only wear black?

Black for me simply says
    let me be.

CHANGE

N ow more than ever
   patience is necessary
   hate to hope takes time

Coin Collection

B
lue books with multiple holes, not holy
holes small, medium, large
the smallest most valuable, oddly

holes awaiting portraits
of Lincoln, Jefferson, Roosevelt
some waiting for rarities like
Mercury, or buffalo replacing Monticello

from a city a mile high
from a city of brotherly love
from a city with a Golden Gate so high
they come to fill the holes

my collection filling the holes
years of sorting through dresser tops
change no longer left askew

then came the ice cream truck

IF ONLY

To be able to see
once again thru the eyes
of a child

to be fascinated by
such simple things
the shape of a block
the bounce of a ball

to be innocent of life
no fear, no preconception
in awe of all that is
around us, a blank slate

eager to explore everything
each taste new
each day a wonder

no thought of difference

EVERYTHING I KNOW, I LEARNED IN THE CAR BUSINESS

There is an ass for every seat
    so, get off yours and meet and greet

If his mouth is moving, he's a liar.
    you never know who will be a buyer

never let a buyer walk out the door
    they might say they'll be back

but there is no be-back bus, for sure
    This one says he is just kicking tires

surely a sign this one is a buyer
    reel them in, get them inside
    forget whatever you promised outside

they always say they want a certain color
    give them a deal and they will take another

. . .

He says he needs to talk to the wife
    ask him, "Is she the boss of your life?"
       I tell you what, I'll have my wife call yours
    and you and I can go out and get a couple beers
    Surely, you don't need yours to decide,
    be a man, have some pride.

What will it take to make a deal today?
    imagine you in your new car driving away

forget your old car, it'll be a down payment
    easy monthly payments, that won't make a dent

in your budget. all you have to do is sign
    sign right here on the bottom line,

it's time to get you in the driver's seat.

FALSE LOVE

You said you loved us
    you said you loved us
    so much you gave up your son

really! do you even exist?
    are you truth or just myth?

my eyes scan this globe
    you supposedly created
    and what do I see?

floods, famine, fires.
    desperation, starvation,
    aggravation, and separation

those who claim you as their own
    hateful, judgmental,
    as hypocritical as any pharisee

. . .

if love is putting others
    above self, then they nor
    you are love

FLAMES OF PASSION

F lames of passion quenched
　　embers still glowing
　　time ticking

wounds that had been healed
　　scars not disappearing
　　too readily exposed again

what was once forgiven
　　too easily remembered
　　becoming a wedge

words no longer valued
　　emotions suppressed
　　has the fire become a pyre?

before darkness overwhelms
　　love thought lost, revives
　　fanned by hope, by understanding

. . .

a small flame flickers
    no true love can ever fade
    flames of passion return.

THE SNUB

We saw the post
                you posted
you were less than
                an hour's drive away

Not just for a quick visit
                but for three days!

The two of you were smiling
                in the picture you posted

You captioned it, "Celebrating
                with family and friends"

We were not invited no
                did we even know you were here

We gather that means we no
                longer fit either category

We are not sure what we
                or either of us did

To deserve the snub but message received.

FORGIVENESS

A man came into our town
    promising a chicken in every pot
    I snuck a peek into his cart
and nary a chicken I found

our town had been in a four-year drought
    the man said he could make it rain
    just how, he could never explain
we waited but there was never a drop about

he told us why there was no rain
    and why no chicken in every pot
    he said among us there was rot
and only he could remove the stain

the stain he said was those not like him
    and they needed to be cast out
    and it was up to us to carry this out
if our town was ever to be whole again

some people believed this type of speech

our town divided as people took sides
each feeling superior, busting with pride
thinking prosperity and wealth almost in reach

some armed themselves with rifles and guns
others marched in the streets
neither side willing to compromise, to meet
and talk, to end what had begun

things grew tense with fear in command
the man kept fueling the flames
he ridiculed one side, calling them names
something had to be done for our town to stand

just as things seemed dark and dire
a stranger rode into our town
he looked around and told everyone to calm down
he had come to help, to put out the fire

of hate and division that choked our town
he said the man was known far and wide
for being a con, a snake who lied
he fed off of people he could put down

the town listened knowing his words were true
coming together they cast the con out
blaming themselves for being filled with doubt
forgiving each other, the right thing to do.

IKIGAI

There is an intersection in life
  not many reach
    life is full of lessons but
  one we seldom teach

we are rarely told to
    follow our dreams
    to do what we love
    is rare it seems

the masses toil in life
    with jobs they hate
    to change to what we love
    often, we find, it's too late

for those who are good at
    and love what they do
    that intersection in life
    is a rarity too.

GOLF

The way a person plays golf reveals a lot
how they react to an errant drive tells a lot
every missed putt reveals their inner self

more of a person's true self comes out
any time things don't go as they planned
shots amiss can bring out the inner demon

the true character usually hidden by societal
ethics that demand calm and control

revelation of their personality is exposed
so, if you want the true measure of a person

play golf

INSIGNIFICANT

As I sit in my chair
    looking out the window
        in the early morning while
the sun is still asleep
I see one lone star
shining in a clear sky

my thoughts move to just
    how insignificant we are
    in the massive universe

but then I think does
    insignificance pay the rent
    or buy my groceries or
    pay for my health care?

does insignificance pay
    my property tax or my
    dental bill or put gas in my car?

suddenly I realize

as I sit in my chair
looking out the window
in the early morning while
the sun is still asleep
insignificance is insignificant

LOVE

The paper tells the story
　　　one repeated over time
　　　two having spent a life
　as one choosing to now
　leave this earth together

this is love

after years of devotion
　　life is taken from only one
　　within days, no more than a week
　　the other succumbs
　　they rejoin

this is love

Loss

The life within you has died,
a spark never igniting

possibilities erased, dreams unfulfilled
joy turning to sadness

a harsh reality that although your first,
may not be your last

even knowing you are not alone
fails to ease the pain

your body asks why
your mind knows not to ask

no one or no thing is to blame
nature simply saying not yet

. . .

but still the heart is weighed down
    the grief no less

so now what do you do?
    seek Isis or Kokopelli,
    or maybe Akna to begin anew.

LOVE AND LUST

I s there a difference between
        love and lust?
            Lust stirs the heart while
love can break it.
One coin, two sides, love
is heads, lust is tails
or maybe lust is in our head
while love is in our heart.

Lust may grab our attention
        but 'tis love giving us dimension
        Lust may wane as years go by
        while love deepens between you and I
        Lust can destroy love with
        the blade of distrust,
        yet love can heal the wounds
        brought on by lust

Maybe, like a stew a good chef can fashion,
        love and lust combine
            to bring life passion.

                            . . .

And passion never dies.

LOVE OF COUNTRY

For the love of country,
　　a noble cause,
　　　without pause
to defend from every enemy

for the love of country
　　willing to compromise
　　see thru the other's eyes
　　so that all better off will be

for the love of country
　　setting aside our differences,
　　actually coming to our senses
　　realizing we are an us not just me

for the love of country
　　there is a better path
　　of love, not hate or wrath
　　'tis time for us all to agree.

MERINGUE

Why is it that meringue is now passé?
    Was it that hard to make, to create?

Chocolate meringue pie a thing of the past
    meringue cast aside for Reddi-Whip

Who makes banana pudding anymore?
    Wafers, custard, bananas, and meringue.
    A Southern delight, like catfish or hush puppies.

MEANT TO BE

It seemed at first
      our love was not meant to be
      even how we met
   not planned or foreseen

the gods or Fate, whatever
     oversees such things
     placing obstacles in our path
     a test, or were they just being mean?

what Fate and the gods forgot
     not just that love conquers all
     but Destiny had set in motion,
     the path for our love, before the fall,

long before the rest of creation
     was brought forth into the light
     long before the stars and the moon,
     only to be awakened when the time was right

. . .

seeds of love planted long ago
  patiently waiting nestled in the ground
  waiting to blossom, to grow
  now in full bloom as each other we found

MEMORY

Symbols of the past released
soaring out over the ocean
a new path before us

a memory held dear

secret glances, cryptic messages
passion igniting giving them
something to talk about

a memory held close

in the light stealing time
moving to the dark side of the street
the world narrowed to only us

a memory made to last

. . .

summers and winters have passed
    some memories have faded
    some chosen to forget

the memory of why now eternal

MISHAP AT HANFORD

This was not just any old accident
    this accident was nuclear
    radiation spewing as someone forgot
a valve left open from a distraction
someone's mind had wandered
something that happens to all of us, every day
oddly, the phone lines in the area went out
at the same time. a coincidence
that boggles the mind

The news reported the incident across the nation
    the mind imagining total destruction, Hiroshima
    and Nagasaki all rolled into one
    people calling could not reach loved ones
    the mind created images too terrible to describe
    we in the city were unaware, our minds were
    focused on daily chores, errands, shopping
    as reports came in things were under control
    disaster avoided, nothing to fret about
    the outside world's imagination creating chaos
    finally the phones were back, my mother called
    "are you okay? are you out of your mind living so
    close to death?"

"No big deal," I said, "and if you don't mind
we are on our way out to dinner!"

ODE TO BLACK

B erry. Beard. Belt. Ball.
    Night. Hole. Heart. Jack.
    Snake. Panther. Rose. Sheep.

Smith. Licorice. Eyed peas.
    Arts. Magic. Ops. Forest.
    Ice. Sea. Widow. Knight.

Lives. Slaves. Race. Tar. Hearse

PARDON?

I am sorry for not remembering
    what you said
      it wasn't that I didn't hear you
I just wasn't listening

It wasn't that what you said was
    not important enough to stick
    after all my brain is full of insignificant
    facts, like Ty Hardin playing Bronco Lane

ODE TO BLUE

B irds. Beards. Bells. Balloon.
    Berry. Bayou. Blanket. Bowl.
    Bonnet. Boy. Bruise

Gunpowder Irish Gin Bottle.
    Mood. Sad. Suede Shoes

Sky

Ocean. Whale. Heron.
    Deep sea. Sea glass.

Eyes

Uniform. Angels. Ribbon. Flame.
    Lives. Grass. Easter Egg. Ink.
    Australian cartoon dog.

My eyes that you lose yourself in

PASSING

Circles of light
    moving thru space
    thru time

passing universe
    after universe
    drawn upward

as if by a black hole

energy of life
    no longer bound
    to earth, humanity

sadness, grief
    judgement forgotten

light no longer
    hindered by dark

life transformed
by death

into brilliance

ELEGY FOR CLYDE

How many hours were spent
    sitting in your armchair

How many baseball games were
    watched on the TV across the room

How many cigarettes were
    crushed out in the ashtray beside you

How many times did you laugh
    at Andy Griffith or Jed Clampett

How many practical jokes did
    you play on your wife

How many times did I fail to
    meet your expectations

            . . .

How many times did you not
    say I love you

How many times have I looked in
    a mirror and seen your reflection

RECHARGING

T he sound of the waves
        the sound of the gulls
        sand changing shape daily

sun reflecting like diamonds
        moon lighting the surf
        the seal that greats the morning

the grace of the dolphins
        the dance of the sanderlings
        oblivious to the chaos of the world

regardless of all else
        walking along the shore
        my mind relaxes, resets,

recharges.

REGRET

How can words express hurt?
　　　not the hurt of a physical wound
　　　but the hurt caused to another's heart

a hurt one had thought had been healed
　　　by the salve of forgiveness and time
　　　only to discover it is a memory
　　　hiding in the back corner of the mind
　　　waiting to show itself without warning

a hurt that mars what one thought
　　　was a love, a connection, unbreakable
　　　a seed of doubt that becomes a weed
　　　with tentacles choking out trust

a dark cloud appearing suddenly
　　　eclipsing the brightness of a clear day
　　　a hurt words cannot heal or remove
　　　now forever a scar across her soul

THANK YOU,
RED WING

You came to me on wings of love
sadly, not of my inspiration but
that of Kincaid as he trod the
bridges of Madison County, where he

too fell in love with another man's wife,
and I thank you.

you have stayed with me over the years
carrying me through the good and the bad
helping me to stand tall in the face of it all

I regret not caring for you as much as
I should and now you sit alone

you were with me as I took my first steps
onto the beach we would soon call home
and now in that home you sit in the dark

in the beginning I did keep you supple

making sure you looked your best, but
    as the years passed, I took you for granted

although your laces failed several times
    you remained strong, unmarred by time

when I leave this world my one request
    will be that you accompany me

who knows what hills will be there to climb,
    as in my Red Wings I step into eternity.

THE CONCRETE SHIP, APTOS

O nce a place filled with music and laughter
    orchestras played as people danced
    mirth echoed across the water
alcohol flowed like the endless tide

built for a war that was over before
    the ocean could lift its hull
    now forever moored along the shore

the pier that once was the pathway
    now sealed off, wind and tide taking toll
    twisted and stripped the ship, leaving it a refuge
    for the birds of the sea

a silent reminder of times thought
    to be simple and carefree
    now to some an eyesore a relic
    that should be removed

for some a symbol a reminder

nothing truly lasts, enjoy every
moment, one day time and tide
will be all that is left.

THE GREAT BARRIER REEF

Miles from land alone
on a boat of thirty souls

snorkeling above the reef
as divers swim below

they, getting up close
the best of views

while I hovered above
too far to touch

In the silence thinking
this is like life

some enjoy the best
some watching from afar

. . .

the few experiencing life
    the majority floating above

waves tossing us about
    below silence and calm

a barrier of status
    the haves and have nots.

The Night Before
My Death

(M y apologies to Clement Moore)

'Twas the night before my death,
    when all through the house,
    there was nary a movement
    except my tip-toeing spouse.

the night nurse was asleep in a chair
    all of us hoping death would soon be there

my stepdaughters were tucked in the guest rooms
    sleeping soundly beside their grooms
    my granddaughter and grandson were fast asleep
    while both cats curled around their feet

when out front we heard such a roar
    a car pulling up, a knock at the door

. . .

my wife descended the stairs
    to find out just who was there

imagine her surprise and how she was relieved
    standing on our porch, were David, Mike, and Steve

lifelong friends, known as the Somersets
    a high school band that success never met

they had come to see me, to laugh, maybe to cry
    to spend my final hours before the last goodbye

so we all told stories of deeds of the past
    laughing too hard, wishing this would last

as morning broke through, I breathed my last
    a life fully lived, it just ran out of gas.

THE WHY OF Y

You always ask why
would be nothing without y

why can't you decide?
what are you?

you're a vowel, you're a consonant
you started in Egypt as a bird

you always change your sound
as a happy baby or a grey day

once being the y in ye
you hide in a code as
a dash dot dash dash

trying to be fancy as money
instead of cash

. . .

you confuse lie by being lay
    not content to be by but bye

in reality, at the end of the day
    you may have an interesting past,
    but you're only one letter,
    from being last.

TIME

Time changes the physical
the hands of time reshaping
slowly shading to gray

the world sees deterioration
the erosion of what used to be

the eyes of the lover still
only seeing the beauty within

TREES

O nce a year they get trimmed,
        standing like silent sentries blocking
        the view between households. Trimmed
so they stay full and thick and solid,

while they prevent eyes from intruding
        they hide the knowledge of a tragedy beyond.

From my side, I cannot see the grieving widow
        now left to live alone.

TRUE LOVE

S ome say
      to truly love another
         one must
   first love oneself

'tis easy to see flaws
      unless it's us in the mirror

if beauty is in the eye of the beholder,
      then to whose eye am I beholden?
      if the eye is the window to the soul,
      why is my window frosted glass?

mirror, mirror on the wall
      reveal to me my flaws and all

for there is one I love
      above all else,
      to truly love her, help me
      love myself.

WHAT OF LOVE?

What of love has not been written?

Countless ways to describe those smitten
    by Cupid's arrow, piercing the heart.

Remember your first love? That was the start
    of feelings, emotions drawing to another.

Over your lifetime was there only one or others
    that ignited a passion within your soul,

someone who you knew if you were to be whole
    you needed them by your side, someone who

loved you as much as you loved them too?
    They say we come into this world and

· · ·

leave this world alone, but they don't understand
    love brings us into this world and if by chance

we find love in life, our leaving is love in remembrance.

TWO SIDES, ONE COIN

L ove and Trust, the two exist as one
as much as does brightness with the Sun
or as do Moon and Stars with the night

Just as Sun without brightness would dim
and night without Moon or stars just black
Love without Trust could never be right

Trust, as a poet once said, is like a vase,
once broken is never again the same
regardless of the words spoken to repair

Love having lost Trust now shattered
becoming words without passion or with
thoughts of betrayal always in the air

The word Love may still cross the lips
but comes from a broken heart pierced
not by Cupid's arrow, but a Medes' dagger.

No Answer

When does a mist become rain
when does rain recede to a mist

when does fog become a cloud
when does a cloud lay down as fog

there is a line when things change
boy to man girl to woman
smoke and sparks to fire

river to sea sea to shore
are the lines set by nature or
set by some kind of god

Life becomes death
death becomes......

WHO'S FIRST?

I always laugh
  when I stop and think
  of how you always assume
I'll be the first to die

It is my goal in life
  to outlive you so
  It will be me not you
  who is left to cry

If there is a god
  then we would die together
  but since there is not
  it will be one or the other

my love for you will last
  forever and although strong
  to leave you here alone
  to me would be just wrong

. . .

so, with my dying breath
    I hope to say, "I'm on my way"
    to join you wherever you may be
    "I told you so", will be the last
    thing I say.

WHY

S uch a disarming word
  'til it comes out of the mouth
  of a two-year-old

rapid firing a salvo
 seeking the truth of the world
 until in frustration one answers,
 because

Why

a question echoing thru time
 as the suffering Job questioned,
 as even in agony, the only begotten son
 cried out, to only be met with
 silence

Why

ironically, the curiousness of youth

slowly evolves to complacency
as in our later years we simply
accept that's just the way it is,
the adult version of
because.

SINCERELY, THE OCEAN

I see the two of you
    walking along my shore
    you are almost as predictable
as my tides, high and low

it is fun to surprise you
    occasionally with a sneaker wave
    watching you scramble to
    not get completely wet

each morning as you walk
    you stare at me to see
    just what creature I
    might reveal to you

as the sun rises and glistens
    across my body, making
    my waves glow as
    they crash towards you

I like to send a seal

to say good morning and
on a rare occasion maybe
dolphins or whales

just know that each day
when you decide to visit
I will be here, lapping
the shore in expectation

NEWSPAPER

E very day the newspaper appears
    in our driveway.
       Well, not always in the driveway
  and not always appearing

On rainy days it's in a plastic sleeve
    a sleeve not always keeping it dry

one thing it always has is that it
    is encircled by a rubber band.
    each day as I walk back to the house
    I shoot the band onto the neighbor's roof.

most of the time the band lands on the roof
    and after five years the collection is massive

one day as I pulled in the driveway
    the father and son next door were on the roof
    slowly picking up rubber bands

              . . .

the father was admonishing the son
　　the son proclaiming his innocence

I smiled to myself and thought
　　would the headline in tomorrow's paper
　　read, "Father and son injured from fall
　　from roof, having slipped on a mass of rubber bands".

THE SNUB

We saw the post
    you posted

you were less than
    an hour's drive away

Not just for a quick visit
    but for three days!

The two of you were smiling
    in the picture you posted

You captioned it, "Celebrating
    with family and friends"

We were not invited nor
    did we even know you were here

. . .

We gather that means we no
    longer fit either category

We are not sure what we
    or either of us did

To deserve the snub
    but message received.

GULLS

They stand, huddled en masse
    crowded together as though
    it was the fourth of July
on Coney Island.

Oddly enough, they segregate,
    brilliant white clustered on one side
    dull brown on the other.

In a flash, they all lift off
    startled or disturbed by something
    maybe a dog running off leash
    a fisherman cutting a path through the sand
    or simply a noise unexpected, too loud

They rise and fill the sky, darkening
    as if a cloud had blocked the sun
    peacefulness now chaos

How do they keep from colliding?
    There is no synchronization, no murmuration

only random darting from point to point
yet not a brushing of feather to feather

as quickly as they rose, they settle,
   again separated by color and kind
   each back in their proper place

The way the racist of the world
   wish humans could be.

A TRAGEDY OF YOUTH

T he classroom now has one empty chair
    the blond girl in glasses no longer there

our eighth-grade teacher has words to share
    the blond girl in glasses no longer here.

"Linda took her own life", she tells us quietly
    the class sits and stares at this new reality

my hand in the air, I ask why,
    not sure, comes the patient reply

only later do we find the cause of her fate
    her parents refused to allow her to date

at twelve we all had kissed and gone steady
    not crossing our minds that we were not ready

. . .

and finally, the truth, what was really her sin
    she had wanted to date one of the airmen

a twelve-year-old girl out with an eighteen-year-old
    a story from any angle that should never be told

the first of my peers to leave from this life
    but not the last, including my first wife.

THOSE WERE
THE DAYS

I t has been said, so I've been told,
    high school is the best time of life
    maybe that's true for some
cheerleaders, football players, cool kids

but for many of us and especially me
    those years are best forgotten
    so I had to laugh when a voice,
    or should I say text from the past
    came across my computer screen

"Are you the Don Grant that went
    to Armijo High?"

I knew the name of the sender
    but for sure could not remember
    if we had ever sat in a class together

so I said I was and then came the pitch
    she was part of the reunion committee
    and planning a get together soon

. . .

I said I had plans and couldn't make it
    she said if things changed, she hoped I would
    after all our class was such a close-knit group

Close-knit? Like a see-thru sweater
    I guess when you're part of the clique
    you forget those of us who were not

so have a good time, reunite and reminisce
    for me, another reunion I'll just have to miss.

REVOLUTION OF THE
KING AND THE PEOPLE

S ome say dry heat is better
    than heat with humidity.
    When it reaches one hundred twenty
degrees the point is moot.

Sitting under an umbrella
    at a sidewalk café
    (even though in Marrakesh,
    I picture the word Cinzano
    across the front)

Smoking a Camel cigarette,
    like Sgt. Bilko who would walk
    a mile for a camel. His Baldina
    camera in its leather case on the table.
    The one he used to snap a shot
    of a Sirocco just before it covered
    him and all else in dust.

A young Arab man approaches and
    says, pardon me, monsieurs but
    are you Americans?

. . .

Hearing the affirmative answer
    he says, you may want to leave quickly.

Rising, crossing the street, walking
    a few blocks up, an explosion rocks
    the stillness of the morning, looking
    back, the café has crumbled,
    the table and umbrella no longer exist.

My father was lucky having been
    forewarned of this of many attacks
    Moroccans would throw at the French

The year was nineteen-fifty-five and
    soon Mohammad V would return
    as a constitutional monarch.

THE HIT

"Look sharp, feel sharp"
      lines from the ad for Gillette Cavalcade of Sports.

every Friday night was boxing,
    ten round matches of the best.

my dad loved watching,
    I think he boxed a little in his day.

maybe that's where he learned
    the hit that knocked me cold.

ABOUT THE AUTHOR

Donald Grant is a husband, cook, cat lover, high-handicap golfer, and poet. Usually in that order.

Living on the Central Coast of California, most days include a walk along the beach with his wife.

Raised as a military brat, he has lived in various parts of the United States and spent several years in North Africa. During his life he has been an engineer, a minister, and small business owner.

He loves to comment on life and when something attracts his attention, he will add his thoughts to a poem or two.

www.ingramcontent.com/pod-product-compliance
Lightning Source LLC
Chambersburg PA
CBHW010330030426
42337CB00026B/4886